◆ F I R S T ◆ A C T I O N ◆

Swimming

Marit Claridge

Contents

2	Introducing swimming	26	Fun and games
4	First things first	28	Going further
10	Learning the crawl	30	Water safety
14	Learning the breast stroke	31	Swimming awards
19	Learning the back crawl	32	Index
22	Learning to dive		

Edited by Mike Halson and Stella Love
Designed by Anne McCaig
Illustrated by Brian Salmon

Swimming advice by Crystal Palace National Sports Centre
Action photography by Ocean Optics Ltd.

The publishers would like to thank all those who gave their assistance in making this book, and especially Lisa Busby, Donna Carpenter, Yasmin Gabr, Patrick Harrop, Darren Hicks, Carina Southward, Susie Stephenson.

INTRODUCING SWIMMING

Everyone can enjoy swimming, no matter how young or old they are or whether they swim in a swimming pool or in the sea. Some people swim because it is a fun way to keep fit and supple. Some like to join clubs and compete in races while others find that learning to swim leads on to all sorts of other exciting watersports such as water polo, synchronized swimming or even windsurfing, water skiing, scuba diving and many others.

This book shows you how to do the basic swimming strokes – front crawl, breast stroke and back crawl. There are exercises to practise the correct arm and leg movements, and photographs showing you how they fit together into a smooth, continuous movement through the water. There is no real order for learning the strokes, so do whichever one you find easiest.

The last part of the book tells you about diving and suggests some games and acrobatics you can try in the water. There is also a section about going further and playing water polo or doing synchronized swimming and some information about the swimming awards you can work towards.

You will need a grown up who can swim well to help you learn to swim. If your school does not run swimming lessons, go to your local pool and find out what classes they run.

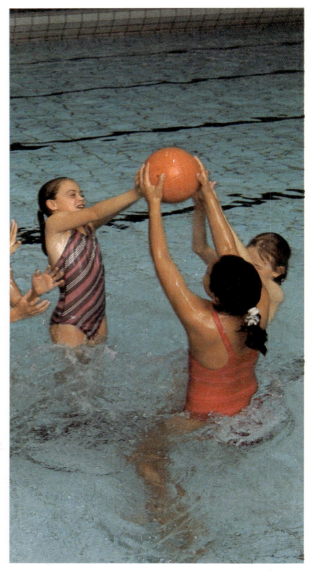

Once you have learnt to swim, there are lots of exciting games you can play.

EQUIPMENT

All you need to go swimming is a costume and towel but you might want to use some of the other things shown on this page. You might use armbands or buoyancy aids when you first start to learn, but floats and goggles can be useful even when you are a good swimmer.

Rinse and dry your costume after use.

Don't forget to take your towel.

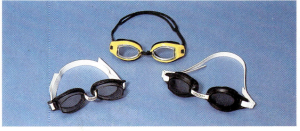

Goggles stop the chemicals (which keep the pool water clean) from stinging your eyes.

A cap keeps hair dry and out of the way.

Floats are often used for training.

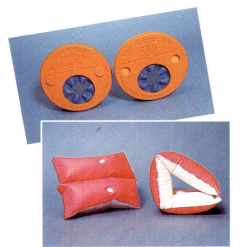

◀ **Armbands and buoyancy aids help you to float when you are a beginner.**

▲
Ball games are fun to play in the pool.

FIRST THINGS FIRST

If you have never been in a swimming pool before, go along and have a look at your local pool. Find out when the pool is very busy and choose a quiet time to go for your first swim. Take your time getting used to the water and just enjoy walking, splashing and jumping in the pool. Later you will learn the basic skills of floating, sculling and gliding.

Entering the pool

Climb BACKWARDS down the steps into the shallow end of the pool. In later visits to the pool, you can try different ways of entering the water. From sitting on the edge, gently lower yourself into the water by twisting round and taking the weight on your hands, as shown in the pictures below. Then stand at the edge and step into the water. Later, try jumping in. You can see how to dive in on pages 22-25.

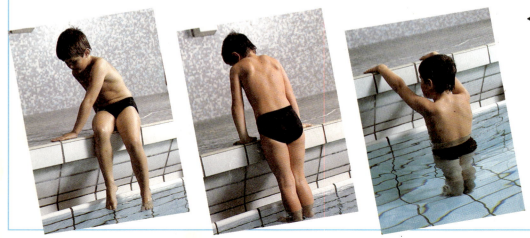

◀ Put your hands across your body onto the side. Turn round, take your weight on your hands and lower yourself into the water.

Climbing out

Try to climb out of the pool without using the steps. Place both hands on the poolside, shoulder-width apart. Push off from the bottom of the pool, and take your weight onto your arms, keeping your elbows high. Straighten your arms and bring one knee up onto the side.

Getting used to the water

Walk around with your shoulders under the water, sliding your feet along the bottom of the pool.

When you feel ready, hold on to your teacher's hands, or the rail at the side of the pool and jump up and down. How high up can you jump?

Learning to float

Take two floats and put one under each armpit. Lift your feet off the bottom of the pool by pulling your knees up towards your chest. Hold your feet up for as long as you can, then put them down again. Repeat this a few times and hold your feet up a little longer each time.

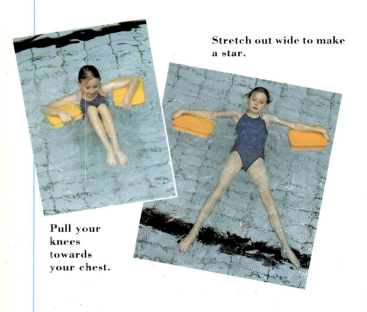

Stretch out wide to make a star.

Pull your knees towards your chest.

Making shapes
See how many different shapes you can make in the water – stretch out your arms and legs as wide as you can to make a star. Stretch your body into a long arrow. Stand up after each shape you make by lifting your head, pushing down on the floats and tucking your legs back underneath your body.

Floating and sculling

When you can float easily using the floats, try again without them. You may find it difficult to begin with, but it will soon get easier.

Stretch your arms out a little way from your sides, with the palms of your hands facing down. Make small, flat figures of eight with your hands and arms to help you get into your floating position and then keep you there. This is called sculling.

You can use the sculling action to move forwards and backwards too. To move head first, scull as before but with your fingers tilted upwards.

To go feet first, scull with your fingers pointing to the bottom of the pool.

Standing up

Without floats to push against you will need to use your arms to help you to stand up.

1 On your front
Press down with your hands as you lift your head and bend your knees. As your body becomes upright, push your feet down and stand. Use your hands for balance.

2 On your back
Lift your head forwards, press down and back with your hands and bring your knees up towards your chest. As you tip forwards give an extra push forwards and up with your hands before pushing your feet down to stand.

Gliding

With a push off from the side of the pool, you can glide on your back and your front.

Front glide

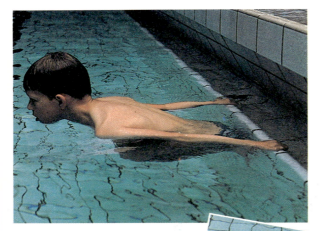

Position yourself at the side of the pool, as shown in the picture.

Push off from the wall with both feet, bringing your arms around in front of your head. Keep your face underwater.

When you have slowed down, stand up as shown on page 7.

Back glide

Holding on to the rail at the side of the pool, place your feet on the wall as shown in the picture.

Let go of the rail and push off with your feet into a glide.

Link-up exercise

Do the following exercise to link up some of the swimming skills you have learnt so far.

Push off from the side of the pool into a glide on your front.

When you stop moving, let your feet drop beneath you. Put your feet on the bottom and stand up.

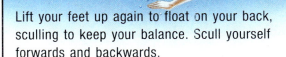

Lift your feet up again to float on your back, sculling to keep your balance. Scull yourself forwards and backwards.

Treading water

Treading water is a useful skill to learn for playing water games and for water safety. When you are ready to swim in deeper water, try floating in an upright position by sculling with your arms and kicking with your feet.

Sit in the water as if you are on a bicycle. Start cycling your legs and scull with your hands flat.

LEARNING THE CRAWL

Body position

Your body should be as flat as possible with your eyes looking forwards and downwards. Your feet should remain just under the surface. Your body will roll a bit during the stroke due to the alternating arm action and breathing.

Entry

Your hand goes into the water, thumb first, arm bent slightly at the elbow. Once in the water stretch your arm and turn the palm of your hand to face your feet.

Pull

Your arm pulls down and back and your elbow bends more until your hand is under your body and your upper arm is at right angles to your body.

Push

Then your hand starts to push backwards and slightly outwards. As your hand pushes back, straighten your arm slowly until your thumb is alongside your thigh.

Arm movements

Your arms take it in turn to pull through the water in a continuous movement. One arm pulls down and back through the water while the other returns to the front, elbow high in the air, to go into the water again.

Leg movements

The main job of your legs in crawl is to keep your body stable and balanced. They take it in turn to kick up and down – one leg is up whilst the other is down. The kick starts at your hips then down through slightly bent knees and ends with a whip-like action of your foot.

Return

Lift your arm out of the water, elbow first. Keep your bent elbow high in the air as you swing your arm forward. Your hand passes close to your head ready to enter the water again.

Timing your breathing

It is important to time your breathing, so it does not spoil the flow of the stroke.

Your head turns as your elbow begins to lift out of the water. Take a quick breath and turn your head back to the front before your arm enters the water. Breathe out slowly into the water.

Crawl leg movements

Start by gliding on your front, holding a float in front of you. Kick your legs up and down, bending a little at the knees, and you will move forwards through the water.

Keep your legs long, toes pointed and try to kick from the top of your legs rather than just your feet. Try also lying on your back and kicking. Hold the float close to your chest or scull with your hands if you can manage without the float.

Dog paddle

Now, without a float, glide on your front. Stretch and pull your arms back under your body at the same time as kicking your feet. Your hands should feel as if they are pushing the water backwards, underneath and behind you.

Stretch and pull ▶

Keep your hands under ◀ the water.

Crawl arms

On pages 10 and 11 you can see how the arms move in crawl. The best way to start learning is as shown below.

Stand at least waist deep in the water, with one foot in front of the other. Lean forward and practise the complete arm movement.

Now push off from the side of the pool and start kicking your legs. Do a stroke with each arm. Try again – do two and then three strokes. See how many you can do.

Breathing

In crawl, you swim with your face in the water. To breathe in, you turn your head to one side as your arm is coming out of the water. You can turn your head to either side, whichever feels best.

Practise crawl breathing by standing at the edge of the pool. Stretch one arm out and hold the rail. Lean forwards with your face in the water. Turn your head to the side, away from your arm, and take a quick breath in. Put your face back in the water and breathe out slowly. Repeat until this kind of breathing seems easy to you.

LEARNING THE BREAST STROKE

You may wish to learn the breast stroke before crawl as you can see where you are going and you can keep your head above the water to begin with.

The wedge kick

There are two types of breast stroke kick. The first one is the WEDGE KICK. You can practise this swimming on your front or your back. Look at the pictures, then sit at the side of the pool and try the kick.

▲ Make your feet long and pointed.

▲ Once you have pulled your knees up, turn your feet out.

Now try the kick in the water, using a float. Hold the float out in front and push off into a front glide. See how far you can go in one kick.

From the glide position, bend your knees up and out, bringing the soles of your feet almost together.

Now turn your feet out like a frog, keeping your feet flat.

Kick your legs out to a wedge shape. Push your heels back, bringing your legs together to point your toes.

Next, practise the kick again, but on your back. Hold one float under each arm and look at your feet.

Arm movements

There are two kinds of arm action in breast stroke – STRAIGHT ARM and BENT ARM. First of all, practise the straight arm action in shallow water, with your shoulders just above the surface. Start by holding your arms out in front, in the glide position, with your hands flat.

With your arms straight, pull them down and back underwater to a wide V-shape.

Bend and drop your elbows and move your hands together.

Stretch out into the glide position again.

Now try linking these movements. Push off from the side into a front glide. As your elbows drop, your knees start bending up. Kick your legs and stretch your arms out to glide.

Body position

Your body should be as flat as possible. This is easier if you put your face in the water while you are gliding.

Leg movements

The second type of kick is called the WHIP KICK. It is faster than the wedge kick and is used in swimming races.

Both types of breast stroke leg kick are strong and should give you a big push through the water.

Whip kick
The whip kick works like the wedge kick, but when your knees are bent it does not look so frog-like. Start in a glide position.

Arm movements

The arm action in breast stroke is a non-stop circling movement with a short glide. This can be done with straight or bent arms. On page 15 you started with straight arms. The bent arm action is faster and goes best with the whip kick.

Bent arm action

Begin with your arms stretched out in front of you, hands touching.

Start pulling your arms out and back, bending your elbows as you do so.

Bring your hands back together in a prayer position and stretch out smoothly into a glide.

Bend your knees down. Bring your heels up to your bottom, hip-width apart, and the soles of your feet to the surface.

Turn your feet out. Keeping them flat, push mainly backwards in a slight curve. Finish by pointing your toes.

Putting the stroke together

Bring your heels up towards your bottom whilst your arms are pulling back. Kick your legs just as your arms move back into the glide position.

Legs begin to kick back, as arms stretch into glide.

Breathing

If you wish, you can keep your head out of the water all the time in breast stroke. But if you do put your face in the water for most of the stroke it will help you swim faster.

▲
Lift your head and breathe in after you have pulled your arms back.

▲
Put your face in the water and breathe out as you push your hands back into the glide position.

LEARNING THE BACK CRAWL

Back crawl is very like front crawl. Your arms take it in turns to pull through the water, balanced by the up and down leg kick.

Start learning back crawl by pushing off from the side into a back glide. Kick your legs up and down. Scull with your hands to keep your balance. Or, if you prefer, hold a float against your chest.

Kick your legs from the hips.

Back crawl arms

Look at the pictures of back crawl arm movements on the next page. The best way to learn them is to start off in a back glide kicking your legs. Try bringing each arm, in turn, up over your head and back through the water like a windmill. Keep practising and see how many arm pulls you can do.

▲

Keep the continuous action going so that one arm is opposite the other all the time.

With back crawl, your face is out of the water all the time. The only problem is that you can't see where you are going – so always have a good look before you set off.

Leg movements

The leg kick used in back crawl is the same as for front crawl. The kick helps to keep your body flat and it balances the strong arm pull as well as pushing you along.

Arm Entry

Your hand and arm stretch behind your head and enter the water in line with your shoulder. Your hand enters little finger first, palm out.

Arm movements

There are two kinds of arm pull you can use in back crawl – STRAIGHT ARM and BENT ARM. Start by learning the straight arm one but the bent arm pull is faster, so you will need to learn this method if you wish to enter swimming races. Your arms enter the water the same way for both pulls.

Keep your head back in the water.

Bent arm pull

As you pull your arm through the water, your elbow bends. Then push your hand towards your feet stretching your arm straight. Lift your arm from the water, thumb first and return it to the entry position.

Straight arm pull

When your hand enters the water, little finger first, your arm is stretched behind your head. In the water your arm stays straight, pulling down and back. Push with your hand, towards your hip until the arm is straight down your side. Lift it, thumb first, out of the water and swing it up over your body ready to enter again.

Keep your body as flat as possible.

LEARNING TO DIVE

Diving can be fun as a sport in its own right as well as a way of getting into the water. Once you can swim in deep water you are ready to learn how to dive.

Putting your head underwater

By now you should be used to putting your face in the water. Before you start diving, try these exercises to see what it's like having your whole head below the surface.

SAFETY

- Make sure you know which is the deep end and only dive at that end.
- Never dive into rivers or gravel pits as they might be shallow or full of dangerous objects.
- Protect your head by holding your hands as shown on the next page.

Hold on to the rail with one hand, take a deep breath and put your face right down into the water. Blow out lots of bubbles.

Push off from the side and glide to the bottom of the pool. Surface by raising your arms and pointing your hands upwards.

You can also try picking up objects from the bottom or swimming through someone's legs.

Sitting dive

Sit on the side of the pool with your feet together and resting on the rail at the edge. Bend forwards with your head down between outstretched arms. Lean forwards and you will topple over into a shallow dive.

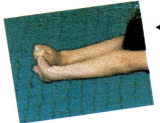

◄ When preparing to dive, link your hands together above your head, as shown in this picture.

Kneeling dive

Kneel down on one knee and curl the toes of your front foot round the edge of the pool. Stretch your arms up over your head and lean forward until you overbalance. Aim for the bottom of the pool and stretch your legs out behind as you go into the water. Glide back to the surface.

Crouch roll

Stand on the side of the pool with your feet together and your toes curling over the edge. Bend your knees and crouch down low.

Stretch your arms over your head, keeping your hands linked, and tuck your chin down on to your chest. Roll forwards and reach for the bottom of the pool.

Pike fall

Stand at the side of the pool with your feet together and toes gripping the edge. Keep your legs straight and bend at the waist. Press your arms close to your ears and hold your hands together.

Lean forward keeping your legs straight and eyes fixed on the water. Stretch your legs out behind you as you enter the water.

▲
Keep your head between your arms.

▲
Legs straight and toes pointed.

Springing dives

In springing dives, you push with your legs to dive into the water instead of toppling your body forwards as before. Try first doing a springing dive from a crouch position.

Crouch dive

Stand up straight with your toes curled over the edge of the pool. Stretch your arms up over your head and link your hands. Bend your knees, keeping your bottom tucked in.

Fix your eyes on the spot where you will enter the water. Spring up by straightening your legs and pushing off with your toes. As your hands touch the water, stretch your legs out and feel all the muscles in your body stretch as hard as they can.

Spring header

When you can do the crouch dive, try a "spring header". Begin with your legs straight and then bend, straighten and push off into the dive.

FUN AND GAMES

You can have a lot of fun trying out different ways of moving in the water, swimming to music and playing games such as ball. Try some of the ideas on these two pages in addition to practising your strokes. See also whether you can invent new strokes of your own.

Playing ball

You can play ball games in the pool as a complete beginner, keeping your feet on the bottom, or as a good swimmer in games such as water polo.

As a beginner, play catch with your teacher. If the ball lands out of your reach, try pushing off from the bottom of the pool and gliding on your front to get it. Kick your legs as they lift off the bottom. If you are swimming with friends, try "pig in the middle".

Once you can swim, play catch in the water where you are just out of your depth. You will need to tread water (see page 9) when you are throwing or catching the ball. If you find this easy, see if you can throw and catch using one hand only. Can you swim keeping the ball out of the water?

If you enjoy playing ball games in the water, you could ask at your pool whether there is a water polo beginners team that you could join.

Water acrobatics

Try doing handstands on the bottom of the pool and somersaults under the water. The water will support your body, which makes these simple gymnastics much easier to do in water than on land.

Handstands
Do handstands in fairly shallow water. Take a deep breath, bend at your waist and reach for the bottom of the pool. Put your hands on the bottom, throw up your legs and stretch. See if you can walk on your hands along the bottom of the pool.

Somersaults
You can somersault forwards or backwards. To go forwards, float on your front, draw your knees up to your tummy and tuck your chin on to your chest. Pretend you are turning a skipping rope backwards and use your hands to paddle yourself round.

To somersault backwards, float on your back and get into the same tucked position as before, only this time turning backwards. Press down with outstretched hands and "skip" forwards.

GOING FURTHER

On pages 26 and 27 you can see how to play ball games and do simple acrobatics in the water, even before you can swim well. As your swimming gets better there are lots of other water sports you may want to try, (see opposite).

Below, you can find out a little about synchronized swimming and water polo. If you want to find out more, ask at your local pool for information on classes and training. Ask too if there is a swimming team or diving club you can join or other clubs where you can take part in such activities as canoeing, snorkelling or life-saving.

Synchronized swimming

Synchronized swimming is performing ballet-like movements and gymnastics in, on and under the water, in time to music. You can do it on your own, with a partner or with a team of people.

Each swimmer needs to control every stroke very carefully, sometimes swimming quickly, sometimes slowly, or treading water and making it all look graceful and easy. The music helps everybody to keep together and it is even played under the water so the swimmers can keep in time when they are below the surface.

Water polo

Water polo is a goal-scoring ball game played by two teams in a swimming pool. There are seven players in each team, including the goalkeeper. The object is to throw the ball into the other team's goal.

The ball can be pushed or thrown but you may only touch it with one hand and your feet must not touch the bottom. Only the goalkeeper can use both hands and stand to throw the ball.

World of Sports Photos

▲ Water skiing

▲ Surfing

▲ Scuba diving

▲ Snorkelling

◄ Windsurfing

▲ Canoeing

WATER SAFETY

Accidents can happen, even to very good swimmers, but if you follow a few simple rules when you are at the pool, at the seaside or near rivers, canals and lakes you can help stop accidents happening and enjoy the water in safety.

At the pool

Don't run by the pool.
You might slip and hurt yourself or knock a non-swimmer into the water.

Don't push people in.
They may not be able to swim, or they might bang their head on the side or hurt someone by landing on them.

Don't push people or hold them under water.
You might scare them, or choke them.

Don't eat sweets or chew gum when swimming.
If they stick in your throat you might choke and get into difficulties.

Do make sure there is no one in the way before you jump or dive in.

Outside

Don't ever swim alone.
If you have problems, strangers might not notice.

Don't fool around near rivers, lakes, canals or quaysides.
If you fall in, it may be very difficult to get out again.

Don't play with rescue and safety equipment.
Someone may drown if it is missing or damaged.

Do wear a life jacket if you go out in a small boat.

Do take care when using air beds and inflatable boats.
Strong winds and tides can sweep you out to sea very fast.

SWIMMING AWARDS

There are lots of different swimming awards you can work towards in your lessons. The Amateur Swimming Association (ASA), The Swimming Teachers' Association (STA), and the Royal Life Saving Society (RLSS) are three of the organizations who run award schemes and below you can see just some of the badges you can earn.

If you have started diving, playing water polo or doing synchronized swimming you will find that there are badges for all of these skills and as your swimming gets stronger you can learn how to rescue people from the water and get your life-saving badges too.

The awards are for every level of swimmer. Some test how far you can swim, some test your speed or style or water safety and some test all your skills in the water.

Your swimming teacher or the swimming coach at your local pool will be able to tell you about the awards you can take and will suggest which one you are ready to work for.

INDEX

armbands, 3
arm movements
  back crawl, 19, 20, 21
  breast stroke, 15, 17
  crawl, 10–11, 13

back crawl, 19–21
back glide, 8
ball games, 2, 3, 26
bent arm pull
  breast stroke, 17
  back crawl, 21
body position
  breast stroke, 16
  crawl, 10
breast stroke, 14–18
breathing
  breast stroke, 18
  crawl, 11, 13
buoyancy aids, 3

canoeing, 29

cap, 3
climbing out of the pool, 5
costume, 3
crawl, 10–13

dives
  crouch dive, 25
  crouch roll, 24
  kneeling dive, 23
  pike fall, 24
  sitting dive, 23
  spring header, 25
  springing dives, 25
diving, 22–5
dog paddle, 12

entering the pool, 4
equipment, 3

floating, 6
floats, 3, 6, 12, 14, 15, 19
front glide, 8

games to play, 26
getting used to the water, 5
gliding, 8
goggles, 3

handstands, 27

leg movements
  back crawl, 20
  breast stroke, 14, 15, 16, 17
  crawl, 11, 12
link-up exercise, 9

making shapes, 6

putting your head under, 22

safety, 22, 30
scuba diving, 29
sculling, 6
snorkelling, 29

somersaults, 27
standing up, 7
straight arm pull
  back crawl, 21
  breast stroke, 15
surfing, 29
swimming awards, 31
synchronized swimming, 28

towel, 3
treading water, 9

water acrobatics, 27
water polo, 28
water skiing, 29
wedge kick, 14–15
whip kick, 16–17
windsurfing, 29

William Collins Sons & Co Ltd
London · Glasgow · Sydney · Auckland
Toronto · Johannesburg

First published 1990
© text William Collins Sons & Co Ltd 1990

A CIP catalogue record for this book is available from the British Library.

ISBN 0 00 190083 8 (HB)
ISBN 0 00 191214 3 (PB)

All rights reserved.

Printed in Portugal by Resopal